T0064546

What I Do Know Is...

What I Do Know Is...

The Truth as I Know It

SHERRIE RAQUEL

authorHOUSE®

AuthorHouse™
1663 Liberty Drive
Bloomington, IN 47403
www.authorhouse.com
Phone: 1 (800) 839-8640

Published by AuthorHouse   08/27/2015

ISBN: 978-1-5049-1945-6 (sc)
ISBN: 978-1-5049-1940-1 (e)

Print information available on the last page.

Any people depicted in stock imagery provided by Thinkstock are models,
and such images are being used for illustrative purposes only.
Certain stock imagery © Thinkstock.

This book is printed on acid-free paper.

NLT
Scripture quotations marked NLT are taken from the Holy Bible, New Living
Translation, copyright © 1996, 2004, 2007. Used by permission of Tyndale House
Publishers, Inc. Carol Stream, Illinois 60188. All rights reserved. Website

CONTENTS

I was led to believe that anyone who was not one of Jehovah's Witnesses was practicing false religion and would be destroyed. I always found that hard to believe.

There are so many different cultures and nationalities of people. We all have different practices and views on religion and worship. Most times we are born into a way of worship or religion adopted by our ancestors, never really choosing at all. There are many things we didn't do as Jehovah's Witnesses. Celebrating birthdays, holidays, voting, pledge of allegiance and displaying the cross are some of the things we did not do.

Since I was only two years old brought into this I just did as I was told without question. There were people that I loved and respected who were God-fearing, loving, kind, good people that were not one of Jehovah's Witnesses. What would happen to the people I love? Especially my very best friend Angela who was all I cared about after meeting her at age 6. I had to know more about what God really requires. Who will be saved and who will not? Would I be destroyed for celebrating birthdays and holidays? Are these things a sin that make God angry? If so, won't it say so specifically in the bible? I had studies with witnesses who directed me to the scriptures to support these beliefs. I realized that I did not always agree with the conclusion they had drawn from the scripture read. Also, since God created all people and all things, surely he understands that most of us are born into our circumstances. Is he not much too great, much too loving, much to merciful to destroy people he created over something for which they had no control? I need to get to know Him better. I have to know more.

So I began to study read, and search for myself to develop my own opinions. Well, when I had to pay a visit to the local ER and the form asked: "what religion are you?" I was stomped. All my life I identified as one of Jehovah's Witnesses, it was all I knew and what I believed. However, I had now gone and gotten baptized at a Baptist church. This disqualified me from being called one of JW's... I think! I finally went with Christian as my answer on the form. This is what started me to really thinking about the different denominations and things that separate us. I realized that these things were not very great or significant at all, for the most part.

DISCIPLINE IN THE CHURCH

Now, one difference of concern was discipline in the church, which seemed nonexistent. The Jehovah's Witnesses however were *very* much opposite and very strict! I never really cared for the thought of even going to church just hearing about the things that were acceptable among them. I worked with a woman who was pregnant by her *married* preacher. She was the secretary and an affair ensued between the two of them. She continued to attend the church sitting proudly on the front row along *with* his **wife and children!** Before, during, and after the pregnancy then *with the baby* once she delivered. This type of thing would **never** be acceptable amongst the witnesses. The witnesses are very much for discipline and keeping the congregation clean. It is very clear in the bible about this. We can read in 1 Corinthians 5:1-12 what Paul says to the church **"I can hardly believe the report about sexual immorality going on among you- something that even pagans don't do. I am told that a man in your church is living in sin with his stepmother. 2: You are so proud of yourselves, but you should be mourning in sorrow and shame. And you should remove this man from your fellowship. 3: Even though I am not with you in person, I am wit you in the spirit. And as though I were there, I have already passed judgment on this man 4: in the name of the Lord Jesus. You must call a meeting of the church. I will be present with you in spirit, and so will the power of our Lord Jesus. 5: Then you must throw this man out and hand him over to Satan so that his sinful nature will be destroyed and he himself will be saved on the day the Lord returns. 6: Your boasting about this is terrible.**

Don't you realize that this sin is like a little yeast that spreads through the whole patch of dough? 7: Get rid of the old "yeast" by removing this wicked person from among you. Then you will be like a fresh batch of dough made with out yeast, which is what you really are. Christ, our Passover Lamb, has been sacrificed for us. 8: So let us celebrate the festival, not with the old bread of wickedness and evil, but with the new bread of sincerity and truth. 9: When I wrote to you before, I told you not to associate with people who indulge in sexual sin. 10: But I wasn't talking about unbelievers who indulge in sexual sin, or are greedy, or cheat people, or worship idols. You would have to leave this world to avoid people like that. I meant that you are not to associate with anyone who claims to be a believer yet indulges in sexual sin, or is greedy, or worship idols, or is abusive, or is a drunkard, or cheats people. Don't even eat with such people. 12: It isn't my responsibility to judge outsiders, but it certainly is your responsibility to judge those inside the church who are sinning. 13: God will judge those on the outside; but as the scriptures say, "You must remove the evil person from among you."

LOVE AND UNITY AMONGST BELIEVERS

One of the purposes of this message is to bring more of GOD'S people together as one. Regardless of Denomination titles all believers united in the common goal of bringing witness of salvation and the love of Christ to nonbelievers. And uniting as one in different ways to accomplish this goal and make each other stronger in fighting the enemy and dealing with evil times we are in together with love until Christ returns. 1 Corinthians 1:10 reads**: I appeal to you dear brothers and sisters, by the authority of our Lord Jesus Christ, to live in harmony with each other. Let there be no divisions in the church. Rather, be of one mind, united in thought and purpose. 1 Peter 3:8-12 reiterates to** *All Christians***: Finally, all of** you should be of one mind. Sympathize with each other. Love each other as brothers and sisters. Be tender hearted, and keep a humble attitude. Don't repay evil for evil. Don't retaliate with insults when people insult you. Instead, pay them back with a blessing. That is what God has called you to do, and he will bless you for it. 10- For the scriptures say, "If you want to enjoy life and see many happy days, keep your tongue from speaking evil and your lips from telling lies. Turn away from evil and do good _Search_ for peace, and work to maintain it. 12: The eyes of the Lord Watch over those who do right, and his ears are open to their prayers. But the Lord turns his face against those who do evil."

SUFFERING FOR DOING GOOD

Since this subject is also in first Peter 3. 1 will address it at this time as well. Verse 13 starts off with the question **"Now who would want to hurt you if you are eager to do good?** Well, as a child and Jehovah's Witness, I witnessed a person be ostracized from the congregation. Ostracized: *To be excluded by general consent from society, friendship, conversation, privileges etc.* Well this person had sinned in some way as we all do as imperfect beings in some form or another at some point in life. However, she was repentant, went to the elders in the congregation to confess, even walking in the rain with her children to make every meeting. I thought when a person repents, confesses, and has remorse that person should be rallied around by the fold given love, counsel and direction. They had a weakness and we as brothers and sisters should lift them up to help make them strong again. We actually drove past this lady in the rain with her children and did not even offer her a ride! Even as a child, I was hurt and thought, this is not love and this is not right. Her own mother had to ignore her. Your own family can't even speak to you or give you a ride. Can you imagine how hurtful and discouraging that can be when you are trying to do the right thing? It hurt me inside and gave me my very first doubt or wonder if this organization really knew what they were doing and if what they were doing was always the right thing. This was the very beginning of my inquisitiveness. See this is the perfect example of the point I want to make here. I think the witnesses were too strict in their discipline and the church too lenient with theirs. If we were all living in Harmony, as we should, I truly believe we could learn from each other and find a median where the truth prevails and things such as discipline could get handled properly, without causing anybody to stumble. My goal is unity among God's true believers acceptance of each other with respect, understanding and love. That is needed in these last and evil days to make us stronger as an entity of righteousness for God through our Lord and savior Christ Jesus. The enemy is plenty busy, and doesn't take a day off. "Separation is self destruction, what's needed is unification."(Tupac Shakur) Anybody ever heard the term "United we stand divided we fall?" This statement is very true. And when I say "we" I mean mankind as a whole! Blacks, Whites, Browns, *every* single human being living on this earth! This is a battle between good and evil and we are the pieces of the game so to speak. It's your decision which side you choose, and evil *never wins.*

THE MEDIA

We are in the middle of a spiritual warfare and really need to remember that during these last and evil days. We have so much pressure and influence from the media we *must* be more aware. Knowledge is power and we desperately need to seek to arm ourselves with the truth and use common sense to see beyond the surface; instead of allowing ourselves to be manipulated into whatever they want us to believe and how they want us to feel, and their greatest goal, how they want us to *act.* The first step to solving any problem is to first recognize that there *is a problem.* Did you know that media stands for multi ethnic destruction in America or manic European devils in action? The media is evil and manipulative. They have gone so far as to study the affects of different frequency on our brain and our emotions, and use these frequencies in music and video games to null us, and our children to a state of unconsciousness and even violence so that we won't think and see what's going on around us or react. They also use television shows like Empire and Scandal and I like some of these shows as well, but they have very subtle undertones and subliminal messages they use to not only insult us in our faces. But to also create diversion, which is the *primary strategy*. Just pay attention. I myself think boondocks are very entertaining and funny, however it is racist, stereotypical and downright buffoonery. Such as, the Black Uncle Tom who hates his own kind but kiss ass for the whites. It's insulting and right in our faces as they get rich and keep us distracted as they kill off our black men. Everyone won't see, believe or understand, and that's okay. I think I realized my gift (as mentioned in scripture later) that God gives all of us. I had an overwhelming desire and feeling to write all my life. I love it I need it. It nags me, stifling me, suffocating me when I can't; makes me unable to keep up with time when I don't write, a day can seem like a week because my mind has covered so much ground and moving so fast per second it seems. So I am writing, if I reach one person I will consider it a success. In this life we should strive "each one to reach one, each one teach one." We are blessed and expected to be a blessing to someone else as often as we see the opportunity to do so. I have a gift of vision too that I just can't explain. I have gotten people very angry with me because of this vision because I can't always explain *how I know*. But if I say I know trust me. I have learned to speak on things I see ahead with my children and close family if it's bad enough. Otherwise I just pray for them. Most like to just call me crazy, as we often do when we don't understand something or someone, which I find insulting and dismissive but it doesn't bother me like it used too, as I grow to a greater consciousness of myself.

THE WISDOM OF GOD

I was led to these scriptures. Some of them were not even listed in the reference section. This lets me know that the message is approved of and guided by God. I want to use as little of my own words and understanding as possible and give you God's message, as HE would have me deliver it and give glory to HIM. **The Cross** has always been a topic of confusion in my mind. As JW's we did not wear or display the cross in any shape form or fashion I was told because it was a thing of humiliation to Christ Jesus, then I was told that's like getting shot then putting the gun up on your wall. Well I saw a show where the man *proudly displayed the gun he was shot with on his wall.* So at that time I realized that could be viewed in different ways just depends on the individual. So I decided to search and see exactly what the bible has to say, about the cross. I was lead to 1Corinthians 1:17 reads: **For Christ didn't send me (Paul) to baptize, but to preach the Good News- and not with clever speech *for fear that the cross of Christ would lose its power.* Verse 18: The message of the cross is foolish to those who are headed for destruction! But we who are being saved know it is the very power of God. Verse 19: As the scriptures say, "I will destroy the wisdom of the wise and discard the intelligence of the intelligent." Verse 20: So where does that leave the philosophers, the scholars, and the world's brilliant debater's? God has made the wisdom of this world look foolish. Verse 21: Since God in his wisdom saw to it that the world would never know him through human wisdom. He has used our foolish preaching to save those who believe. 1 Corinthians 22-31: it is foolish to the Jews, who ask for signs from Heaven. And, It is foolish to the Greeks,** who seek human wisdom. Verse 23: So when we preach that Christ was crucified, the Jews are offended and The Gentiles say it's all nonsense. Verse 24: But to those called by God to salvation, both Jews and Gentiles, Christ is the power of God and the wisdom of God. Verse 25: This foolish plan of God is wiser than the wisest of human plans, and God's weakness is stronger then the greatest of human strengths. Verse 26: Remember, dear brothers and sisters, that few of you were wise in the world's eyes or powerful or wealthy when God called you. Verse 27: Instead, God chose things the world considers foolish in order to shame those who think they are wise. And he chose things that are powerless to shame those who are powerful. Verse 28: God chose things despised by the world things counted as nothing at all, and used them to bring to nothing what the world considers important. Verse 29: As a result, no one can ever boast in the presence of God. Verse 30: God has united you with Christ Jesus. For our benefit God made him to be wisdom itself. Christ made us right with God; he made us pure and Holy and he freed us from sin. Verse 31: Therefore, as the Scriptures say, "If you want to boast, boast only about the Lord." I think these scriptures speak quite plainly for themselves, don't you? The cross has power and no shame affiliated with it according to scripture. Now who can say otherwise?. 1Peter 3:14 continues: **But even if you suffer for doing what is right, God will reward you for it. So don't worry or be afraid of their threats.15: Instead you must worship Christ as Lord of your life. And if someone asks about your Christian hope, always be ready to explain it. 16: But do this in a gentle and respectful way. Keep your conscience clear. Then if people speak against you, they will be ashamed when they see what a good life you live because you** belong **to Christ. 17: Remember,** *it is better to suffer for doing good,* **if that's what God wants, than to suffer for doing wrong!** *18: Christ suffered for our sins once for all time.* **He never sinned, but he died for**

sinners to bring you safely home to God. He suffered physical death, but he was raised to life in the Spirit. 22: Now Christ is gone to heaven. He is seated in the place of honor next to God, and all the angels and authorities and powers accept his authority. I underlined "for all time" on purpose for emphasis sake because, I've heard it said by some that Jesus did not die for people of *this day and time.* Well, all I can do is wonder where they got that information? The scripture is very clear. Is there any doubt or questions on this point? Let's move on.

LIVING FOR GOD

1 Peter Chapter 4

So then, since Christ suffered physical pain you must arm yourselves with the same attitude that he had, and be ready to suffer too. For if you have suffered physically for Christ, you have finished with sin. 2: you won't spend the rest of your lives chasing your own desires but you will be anxious to do the will of God. 3: you had enough in the past of the evil things godless people enjoy - their immorality and lust, their feasting and drunkenness and wild parties, and their terrible worship of idols. This leads me to The *Pledge of Allegiance*. The word allegiance means "loyalty" to stand and face the flag with your hand over your heart is *an act of worship. That's* **Idolatry** *plain and simple*. (Exodus 20:3- 7:) **You MUST NOT have any other GOD but me. You must not make for yourself an idol of any kind or an image of anything in the heavens or on the earth or in the sea. You must not bow down to them or worship them, for I, the Lord your God, am a jealous God who will not tolerate your affections for any other gods.** To love your country is one thing, pledging loyalty to an inanimate object is another! In Exodus 3:14 when Moses asked "who shall I say sent me? **God replied to Moses, "I AM WHO I AM. Say this to the people of Israel: Yahweh, the God of your ancestors—the God of Abraham, the God Of Isaac, and the God of Jacob—has sent me to you." This is my eternal name, my name to remember for all generations. (A NAME, MAY I JUST REMIND YOU THAT WILL TRANSLATE AND CHANGE ACCORDING TO THE LANGUAGE IT IS SPOKEN IN)** In verse 18 he is referred to as **the God of the Hebrews. In** Exodus 6:2 **And God said to Moses, "I am Yahweh—The**

Lord verse 3 **I appeared to Abraham, to Isaac and to Jacob as El-Shaddai -"God Almighty"- but I did not reveal my name, Yahweh, to them." In verse 6 he says "Therefore say to the people of Israel: "I am the Lord." In** Exodus 20:7 **the Lord says: You must not misuse the name of the Lord your God. The Lord will not let you go unpunished if you misuse his name.** This is another subject that seems to bring about debate with Jehovah's Witnesses, and its time to put that to rest as well. He has many names. If being called Yahweh and Jehovah was a must to The Almighty, why would he let time pass and not even reveal his name until asked? Just like we respect the elderly with "ma'am" and "sir" and we respect people in authority such as a judge with "Your Honor" It seems only logical to me that we would show *at least* the same respect and more to the Most High creator of all things. It's good to know this information if we claim to know him. However, I know parents that won't let their children call them by their first name!

But somehow it's ok to call the judge of all judges, the Creator by his first name! I really don't think so. It's a matter of respect and honor. It should or can be used in praise and worship or for teaching purposes to those who don't know. However this is one of those petty details that stand in the way of more important issues. It keeps us divided and focused on *the wrong things*! We will not argue over it any longer at all. Its just part of the distraction method used by the enemy as mentioned before. He refers to 3 different names himself when explaining his name! Of course your former friends are surprise when you no longer plunge into the flood of wild and destructive things they do so they slander you. But remember that they will have to face God who will judge everyone, **both the living and dead. 6: that is why the Good News was preached to those who are now dead- so although they were destined to die like all people, they now live forever with God in the Spirit. 7: The end of the world is coming soon. Therefore, be honest and** disciplined in your prayers. 8: Most important of all, *continue to show deep love for each other, for love covers a multitude of sins!* 9: Cheerfully share your home with those who need a meal or a place to stay.10: *God has given each of you a gift from his great variety of spiritual gifts. Use them well to serve one another!* 11: Do you have the gift of speaking? Then speak as though God himself were speaking through you. Do you have the gift of helping others? Do it with all the strength and energy that God supplies. Then *everything you do* will bring glory to God through Jesus Christ. All glory and power to him forever and ever! Amen.   Sufferingfor being a Christian: *1Peter 4:* 12:So dear friends, don't be surprised at the fiery trials you are going through, as if something strange were happening to you. 13: Instead, be very glad–for these trials make you partners with Christ in his suffering, so that you will have the wonderful joy of seeing his glory when it is revealed all the world. In first Peter four verse19 it reads: So if

you are suffering in a manner that pleases God keep on doing what is right, and trust your lives to the God who created you, for HE will NEVER fail you. I am not sure to whom I may be speaking at this time. This research and study came about mainly as personal research for my own knowledge. Then it occurred to me that there is so much information out there, so many religions, so many denominations, that if nothing else, I would like to leave some clarification for my children and my grandchildren to know the things that I know to be true and the things that I know to be important, and the things they need to know. One very important piece of advise I received was to *fight your battles on your knees! Give every person or situation over to Him and just wait!* There will be hard times, heartaches, and pain in every life. You may feel alone, afraid even desperate sometimes. Talk to Him, cry out if you have to or prayer can be a whisper from your heart. Prayer comes from the heart anyway. Also, pick your battles wisely, THINK, Is this person, situation and subject matter going to mean or change anything in my life? If so, is it good or bad? Is it worth your freedom or your life to even validate them with a response? Some people are not worth your attention your words or energy and you don't even have to respond to people just because they are talking to you. As a matter of fact it hurts them more when you ignore them and don't make them relevant. Think before you speak. Life is short and your time is precious because time is something you can never get back. Rejoice and be happy in every single second you can. Pray earnestly, daily and consistently all through the day! If you keep giving praise and thanking Jesus he will supply all your needs. As indicated in previous scripture, we all must suffer in this life just like Christ did. Deal with it, trust God, bend your knees, bow your head pray and keep on praying until something happens. Never give up, never stop believing never stop moving. You may get weary and have to rest, so rest. Then get back to living for God and reaching for all the abundance in life God means for you to have. Raelynn Nelson, Xavier & Shatera Turner, and Terrez Murry. I pray you are paying attention because I am very much thinking of you especially as I write the previous. I love you so much. We are all commanded to love. Please live in unity, peace and love, always being there for one another where one can't fall for the other! Break the cycle in this family. I know you can, you have *that love* because you are my children and you belong to The King. Romans 6:14 **Sin is no longer your master, for you no longer live under the requirements of the law. Instead you live under the freedom of God's grace!** Amen!

PAUL'S MESSAGE OF WISDOM

1 Corinthians chapters 2-3: **When I first came to you, dear brothers and sisters, I didn't use lofty words an impressive wisdom to tell you God's secret plan. For I decided that while I was with you I would forget everything except Jesus Christ, the one who was crucified. I came to you in weakness-timid and trembling. And my message and my preaching were very plain Rather than using clever and persuasive speeches, I relied only on the power of the Holy Spirit. I did this so you would trust not in human wisdom but in the power of God.. Yet when I am among mature believers, I do speak with words of wisdom, but not the kind of wisdom that belongs to this world or to the**

rulers of this world, who are soon forgotten. No, the wisdom we speak of is the mystery of God–his plan that was previously hidden, even though he made it for our ultimate glory before the world began. But the rulers of this world have not understood it; if they had they would not have crucified our glorious Lord. That is what the Scriptures mean when they say, "No eye has seen, no ear has heard, and no mind has imagined what God has prepared for those who love him." 10: But it was to us that God revealed these things by his spirit. For his spirit searches out everything shows us God's deepest secret's. No one can know a person's thoughts except that person's own spirit, and no one can know God's thoughts except God's own spirit (not the world's spirit), so we can know the wonderful things God has freely given us. When we tell you these things, we do not use words that came from human wisdom. Instead we speak words given to us by the spirit, using the Spirit's words to explain spiritual truths. But people who are not spiritual cannot receive these truths from God's Spirit. It all sounds foolish to them and they can't understand it, for only those who are spiritual can understand what the Spirit means. Those who are spiritual can evaluate all things, but they themselves cannot be evaluated by others. For, "WHO CAN KNOW THE LORD'S THOUGHTS? WHO KNOWS ENOUGH TO TEACH HIM?" But we understand these things, for we have the mind *of Christ.*

1 Corinthians Chapter 3*: Paul an Apollos, Servants*: Dear brothers and sisters, when I was with you I couldn't talk to you as I would to spiritual people, I had to talk as though you belonged to this world or as if you were infants in the Christian life. I had to feed you with milk, not solid food because you weren't ready for anything stronger. And you still aren't ready, for you are still controlled by your sinful nature. You are jealous of one another and quarrel with each other. Doesn't that prove you are controlled by your sinful nature? Aren't you

living like people of the world? When one of you says, "I am a follower of Paul," and another says, "I follow Apollos" aren't you acting just like people of the world? After all, who is Apollo's? Who is Paul? We are only God's servants through whom you believed the Good News. Each of us did the work the Lord gave us. I planted the seed in your hearts, and Apollos watered it, but it was God who made it grow. It's not important who does the planting or who does the watering. What's important is that God makes the seed grow. The one who plants and, the one who waters, work together with the same purpose. And both will be rewarded for their own hard work for we are both God's workers. And you are God's field. You are God's building. 3:10-Because of God's grace to me, I have laid the foundation like an expert builder. Now others are building on it. But whoever is building on this foundation must be very careful. For no one can lay any foundation other than the one we already have—Jesus Christ. Anyone who builds on that foundation may use a variety of materials—gold, silver, jewels, wood, hay, or straw. But on the judgment Day, fire will reveal what kind of work each builder has done. The fire will show if a person's work has any value. If the work survives, this builder will receive a reward. But if the work is burned up, the builder will suffer great loss. The builder will be saved, but like someone barely escaping through a wall of flames. Don't you realize that all of you together are the temple of God and that the Spirit of God lives in you? God will destroy anyone who destroys this temple for God's temple is holy, and you are that temple.

1 Corinthians3: 18 **Stop deceiving yourselves. If you think you are wise by this world's standards, you need to become a fool to be truly wise. For the wisdom of this world is foolishness to God as the scriptures say,** "He traps the wise in the snare of their own cleverness."

And again, "The Lord knows the thoughts of the wise; he knows they are worthless." *So don't boast about following a particular human leader. For everything belongs to you– whether Paul or, Apollos or, Peter, or the world, or life and death, or the present and the future; everything belongs to you, and you belong to Christ, and Christ belongs to God.*

So we live in this world of unrest, hate and prejudice against one another for whatever reasons. Why? None of us are responsible for creation and none of us can change what we are created as. You hate your brother or sister because their skin is not the same color as yours? Then you would have to hate the creator, who is both you and your brother's creator. How silly is that to hold a person liable for something over which none of us has any control. I do realize that some people do not believe in God. I personally don't understand that at all but I'm certainly not going to argue with you about it. If you choose to hear my views or have questions I would surely share them and may possibly be curious about why you feel the way you do. But it would definitely not be an argument. A civil conversation, calm exchange of ideas and feelings between two or more people respecting each other makes wonders of difference in how we are received and how we receive others. It leads to contentment and peace. Because I personally believe every one fears who or what they don't understand and we are all different. And fear leads to anger then violence and so on and so forth. One thing I know to be undeniable is that we are all made of flesh and blood and inside, all our flesh and all our blood is exactly the same. For my fellow believers, can we stop fighting over how, who, what, when and where? Romans 8: 18-19 says: *yet what we suffer now is nothing compared to the glory he will reveal to us later. For all creation is waiting eagerly for the future Day when God will reveal who his children really are.* Hmm, If God has not revealed who his children are why do so many think they already know who he will save? He *is* the creator of *all things*. So why does everyone think they can cut him up into fractions to fit him into one particular denomination? He is so much greater than we can even imagine just as scripture says, until it is actually insulting to think the creator of all things in this universe can be put in a box by the very people *He* created! We will all be judged by our individual actions! The scripture is clear as far as I'm concerned. He has not yet revealed who his children are and the details of eternity are unknown. Now what is all the division and conflict about? With all the evil happening in this day God's children need to stick together and pray incessantly everyday for strength, direction, wisdom to keep us from constantly repeating history. Also about our oppressors and abusers we should pray as well. Remember, it's not our battle it's the Lord's, the battle has already been fought and the victory is already won. We know evil *never wins!*

1 John 3:2 tells us that: **He has not yet shown us what we will be like when Christ appears.**

1 Corinthians 8:1-3tells us that: **While knowledge**

makes us feel important, it is Love that strengthens the church. Anyone who claims to know all the answers doesn't really know very much at all. But the person who loves God is the one whom God recognizes.

Ephesians 3:6-12: *And this is God's plan: Both Gentiles and Jews who believe the good news share equally in the riches inherited by God's children. Both are part of the same body and both enjoy the promise of blessings because they belong to Christ Jesus. By God's grace and mighty power, I have been given the privilege of serving him by spreading this Good News. Though I am the least deserving of all Gods people, he graciously gave me the privilege of telling the Gentiles about the endless treasures available to them in Christ. I was chosen to explain to everyone this mysterious plan that God, the creator of all things, had kept secret from the beginning. God's purpose in all of this was to use the church to display his wisdom in its rich variety to all the unseen rulers and authorities in the heavenly places. This was his eternal plan, which* he carried out through Christ Jesus as Lord. Because of Christ and our faith in him, we can now come boldly and confidently into God's presence.

Romans 8:34 reads: **who will condemn us? No one-for Christ Jesus died for us and was raised to life for us and he is sitting in the place of honor God's right-hand, Pleading for us. Can anything ever separate us from Christ's Love? Does it mean he no longer loves us if we have trouble or calamity, or are persecuted, or are hungry, or destitute, in danger or threatened with death? (As the scriptures say, for your sake we are killed every day; we are being slaughtered like sheep.") No, despite all these things, overwhelming victory is ours through Christ, who loved us.**

So the good news is salvation is for everyone. I know we have experienced a lot of injustice lately but the Lord also said **vengeance is his and that which was last will one day be first.** He will handle things far better than any of us could imagine. Believer's please don't argue over how the afterlife will be, who will be saved, what we will be like, who is going to heaven how many going to heaven who and where and what is hell*. Our commandment at this present time is to love one another* And seems that we can barely manage that. So why don't we as believers respect one another, so do not try to force others to adhere to your stipulations, you would hinder other believers by making up rules and standards for how everyone is to behave. Everyone's Jesus in whatever denomination or higher power should be respected. You do not have to agree, it's okay to agree to disagree. In first Corinthians eight and nine Paul talked about freedom of choice on practices not expressly forbidden in scripture.

And please remember Ephesians 6:12- for we are not fighting against flesh and blood enemies, but against evil rulers and authorities of the unseen world, and against evil spirits in the heavenly places. Therefore, **THERE IS NO TIME** for racism, fighting, and killing amongst one another. We need each other to be stronger and more effective in this spiritual battle.

So let's leave details of eternity to God and try to be the best at what he has commanded us to do Today: Love! Period.

LOVE,

SHERRIE RAQUEL

DEDICATION PAGE

This is my beautiful son and daughter Mr. and Mrs. Xavier and Shatera Turner. The proud Christian couple has just announced the October arrival of my very own and very first grandson Xavion Prince-Von Turner. To whom I dedicate this publication. I Love You soo much already and I'm just dreaming of you now

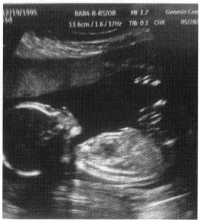

Thursday, April 23, 2015

Thursday, April 23, 2015 "Sexy Sassy Sherrie"
Fabulous 44

My Life

In this life many times you have to walk alone

There have even been times there

was no place to call home

I have been ridiculed and criticized by many

The lines to judge and stone me have

been bountiful and plenty

I started to feel that what they say is true

"Can't you see there's something wrong with you"

But the great comforter held me so tight she rocked

me in her arms and said "everything is alright"

I said I have to ask, is it true what they say,

does the Lord hate people like me

She said "of course not my child why

would you ever think such a thing

Because all the things I know people

say about me

She chuckled and said "oh darling cant you see

You possess such beautiful qualities

And they can't see how you could possibly

Have the very thing that they could never be

what they just cant buy you see, but they just

don't possess the capability, to be what you are

so naturally. No matter what you go through

you see you are still full of genuine love and

honesty. How on earth could this possibly be she's

gorgeous she's blessed she's pure quality!

So yes my dear quite inevitably, they see in you all they

desire to be. Sincerity is what they see in you. And

courage my love, courage to walk, In your own Truth.

DEDICATED TO MY DAUGHTER **RAE LYNN NELSON**

ACKNOWLEDGEMENTS

My mother made this research desirable. Had it not been for Jeanette Pridgeon, her steadfastness and faith in her beliefs I would have never been so curious or determined. My children made this necessary: Rae Lynn Nelson, Shatera VaShae Turner, Terrez Veron Murry. Even the children I did not birth and have grown to love. Jay, Tara and Shirra Brothers, LaShera Shatavia Murry and lil Tave, Terrance Von Murry the second, Xavier Turner, Jeremy and Rayven Nelson, Lakendra Olgesby and my two God-daughters D'Ann(Julia) and D'Cora Dotson and Le'Anna Sneed. If this is nothing to anybody else I would like it too be a guide or words of advise I left just for you guys, my beautiful babies (tears) I Love you so much words could never express. Hopefully this is just part one. I would like to thank my sister Rashunda Jenkins who trusted me enough to go to the church I was attending at the time, to get baptized. I Love you so much and I am soo proud of you and all you have achieved and become. You made me realize it was ok to have questions, want answers and I was not the only one who felt this way. She also made me realize that, I don't have to answer to anybody or be questioned about anything I say, do or feel, I'm grown (smile). Mr. Mark Massey played a big part in that lesson as well and was my muse and inspiration to finish what I started long ago. I don't think he knows the inspiration he has been to me. Thank you old friend. To my baby sister, Crystal Anderson, who understands me more than most, and loves and accepts me just as I am, the peacemaker and tolerant one. My only niece Laila Sheray, you are a very smart and beautiful young lady and auntie loves you very much. Shout out to my wonderful brothers in law Maurice Anderson and Daryl Jenkins. I'm so proud of you guys *and so happy for my sisters, keep loving them. A special thank you to Mrs. Carol Key; a very endearing, strong and nurturing woman who picked me up when I was down and brought me to church. I will never forget. My spiritual sister Ms. Erma Williams, who prayed for me, and my family and pulled me too my knees to pray for myself when I didn't even think to do so. She told me how worthy I was and how much the Lord loves me. I am forever grateful. My aunties wow, Florell Dean,who has always loved and been there for me. She told me when I was wrong but loved me anyway. Wilma Pickens, Benita Pridgeon, Kress Taylor all so special sweet and wonderful to have had all my life. Never denied me a thing always there with love, I love you so much. I have mention Mary Murray in that group a special friend of moms who was just as loving. A beautiful woman inside and out who taught me a whole lot, thank you Mary. A special cousin Tonika Pridgeon Collins who stayed encouraging me, thank you family. To Ebony Murray for much love and support for which I am so grateful. Linda Payne a.k.a, Ky, I Love you girl. Dr. Simmie Armstrong Jr. who saved lives in my family more times than I could count. I would not be here if not for him. Terri Goodwin, my dear friend. Pamela Smith my forever friend and Angela Jackson my souls twin. She can read my mind and finish my sentences. Best Friends Forever. You have all truly been Heaven sent into my life, without all of you, there would be no me. Ronald James my old neighbor and friend, who is an author, thank you for the nudge. If you are reading this It must be okay. (smile). To Mrs. Arlene Woody and Ms. Sandra Davis. These are two beautiful women to whom I always felt some connection and admired from afar learning any and everything I possibly could. I Love you all so very much.*

SHERRIE

Printed in the United States
By Bookmasters